WHERE on EARTH?

# ANTARCTICA

By Shalini Vallepur

Designed by Brandon Mattless

## Photo Credits

All images are courtesy of Shutterstock.com, unless otherwise specified. With thanks to Getty Images, Thinkstock Photo and iStockphoto. Front Cover – Chubarov Alexandr, Lemberg Vector studio, Maquiladora, matrioshka, Tarikdiz, Yaska, focus_bell. Recurring Images – Hollygraphic, Apostrophe, iizuka, Yaska, Maquiladora, StockAppeal, VectorShow, Attitude, Kharchenko Ruslan, winnond. 6–7 – Alexander Lysenko, Denis Burdin, Islarsh, Mradyfist. 8–9 – euphro, Stephen Hudson. 10–11 – Adam C. Jones, Brian L Stetson, CRStocker, Steve Allen, Urbain Joseph Kinet. 12–13 – Brian L Stetson, Tory Kallman, vladsilver. 14–15 – Anton Rodionov, M Rutherford, Tarpan. 16–17 – Liam Quinn, Lomvi2, tanyaya, Tarpan. 18–19 – Vasilyev Maxim, Wayne Morris, Peter Rejcek. 20–21 – deer boy, Georgios Kollidas, Nasjonalbiblioteket. 22–23 – Jason Auch, spatuletail.

Words that look like **this** can be found in the glossary on page 24.

## BookLife
### PUBLISHING

©2021
BookLife Publishing Ltd.
King's Lynn
Norfolk PE30 4LS

ISBN: 978-1-83927-197-7

**Written by:**
Shalini Vallepur

**Edited by:**
William Anthony

**Designed by:**
Brandon Mattless

# CONTENTS

# WHAT IS A CONTINENT?

A continent is a large area of land. There are seven continents on Earth. The continents are surrounded by five oceans.

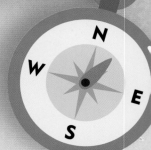

North America

Arctic Ocean

Europe

Asia

Atlantic Ocean

South America

Africa

Pacific Ocean

Indian Ocean

Antarctica

Australia

Southern Ocean

Earth's **population** lives on the seven continents. Each continent has different types of weather, **landscape** and ways of life.

Let's learn about Antarctica!

# WELCOME TO ANTARCTICA!

Where on Earth is Antarctica? Antarctica is the continent that is farthest south. Antarctica does not have any countries. It is split into **territories** that are controlled by different countries around the world.

Antarctica

Southern Ocean

Nobody lives in Antarctica **permanently**. Scientists and workers live in special **research stations** for a short time to learn about Antarctica. People sometimes visit Antarctica to look at the landscape.

Norwegian research station

American research station

# ANTARCTIC WEATHER

The Equator runs through the middle of the Earth. Places that are farther away from the Equator are usually colder than places that are closer to it.

The South Pole is in Antarctica. It is the farthest place south of the Equator.

Equator

Antarctica is one of the coldest and windiest places on Earth. Most of Antarctica is covered in snow and ice all year round. Some snow melts during the summer. **Blizzards** can happen when it gets windy.

Mount Jackson

Snow

Antarctica is called a polar desert because there is very little rain.

# LIVING IN ANTARCTICA

Scientists live in tents for short times.

The scientists who live in Antarctica study its **climate**, animals, plants and rocks. They have to make sure they are dressed properly and keep warm.

Around 3,700 people live in Antarctica during the summer months.

It can be very hard to live in Antarctica because of the weather. Polar night happens during winter and there is usually no sunlight for around 30 days.

The southern lights, or aurora australis, can be seen during polar night.

# ANTARCTIC ANIMALS

The animals that live in Antarctica are specially **adapted** to live in the cold weather.

Emperor penguins have strong claws on their feet to help them walk on snow and ice.

Emperor penguins

Sometimes it's easier to slide around!

Killer whales live in the waters around Antarctica. They have **blubber** under their skin to help keep them warm.

Killer whale

Killer whales are also known as orcas.

Albatrosses have very large wings. These large wings help them to fly a long way to look for food.

Albatross

Seals have large eyes that help them to see underwater and catch **prey**. Like killer whales, seals also have blubber under their skin to help keep them warm.

Seal

# ANTARCTIC PLANTS

Few plants can grow in Antarctica because of the climate. Plants that do grow there are specially adapted.

Antarctic hair grass has long roots to help it stay in place when it is windy.

Hair grass

Antarctic pearlwort grows near the coast where there is more water.

Pearlwort flowers

Pearlwort flowers grow in summer.

On the islands around Antarctica, plant-like moss and **lichen** grows on rocks.

This gentoo penguin has built a nest using moss.

# Fact File:
# ANTARCTICA

There are lots of interesting things on Antarctica's landscape. Let's take a look!

## Fact File:

**Longest river:**
Onyx river
(32 kilometres)

**Tallest mountain:**
Mount Vinson
(4,897 metres)

**Biggest glacier:**
Lambert-Fisher Glacier
(400 kilometres long)

Mount Vinson was discovered in 1957. Since then, it has been climbed by 1,000 people.

Blood Falls is an interesting glacier. It gets its name from its dark red colour.

# EXPLORING ANTARCTICA

Many people have tried to explore Antarctica in the past. The weather makes the journey very dangerous. Many explorers have had to leave Antarctica early because of the weather.

In 1773, Captain James Cook almost became the first person to discover Antarctica.

Nobu Shirase led a trip to Antarctica in 1912 but had to go home because of heavy snow.

In 1911, Roald Amundsen became the first person to make it to the South Pole. The trip was very dangerous. It took two months for his group to reach the South Pole.

Roald Amundsen

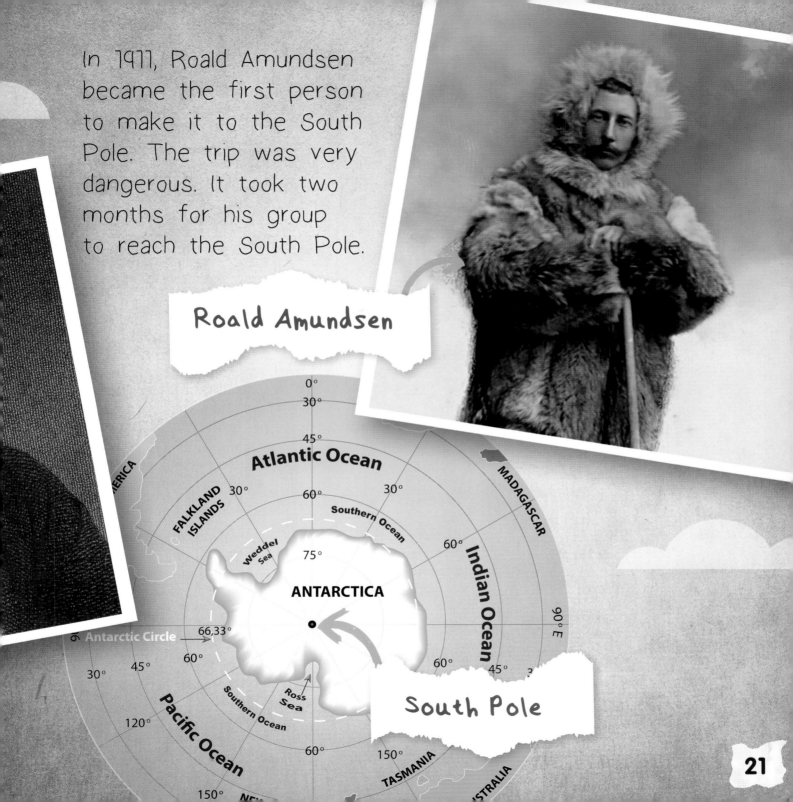

0°
30°
45°
**Atlantic Ocean**
FALKLAND ISLANDS
30°
60°
30°
MADAGASCAR
Southern Ocean
60°
Weddel Sea
75°
**Indian Ocean**
**ANTARCTICA**
90° E
66,33°
Antarctic Circle
60°
60°
45°
30°
45°
60°
Ross Sea
Southern Ocean
**Pacific Ocean**
120°
60°
150°
TASMANIA
STRALIA

South Pole

# CLIMATE CHANGE

Climate change is when the normal climate and weather of an area changes over time. Antarctica is getting warmer because of climate change.

Some of the ice around Antarctica has started to melt because of climate change.

Melting ice and snow will make the sea levels get higher. This could cause floods in other places around the world.

Some animals are in danger of losing their homes because of climate change.

# GLOSSARY

adapted      changed over time to suit the environment

blizzards      heavy snowstorms

blubber      a thick layer of fat under the skin of sea mammals such as whales and seals

climate      the common weather in a certain place

glacier      an extremely large amount of ice that moves slowly

landscape      how the land is laid out

lichen      a plant that grows on rocks and trees and makes food using the Sun

permanently      lasting forever

population      the number of people living in a certain area, such as a city or country

prey      animals that are hunted by other animals for food

research stations      buildings that scientists study in

territories      areas of land claimed by a country

# INDEX